# THE MANAGING ASSESSMENT CENTRES POCKETBOOK

By John Sponton & Stewart Wright

*Drawings by Phil Hailstone*

"An exceptionally practical guide to the complex business of designing and running assessment centres – each step is clearly explained with plenty of hints and tips along the way."
**Pauline Garnett, Group HR Manager, ASD Metal Services**

"A really useful and practical guide – comprehensive, concise and clear. The information is very accessible. It is as relevant, as a reminder of good practice, for those who have run assessment centres before, as it is for anyone considering an assessment centre approach for the first time."
**Sophie Pickup, HR & Development Manager, Northumbrian Water Limited**

*Published by:*
**Management Pocketbooks Ltd**
Laurel House, Station Approach, Alresford, Hants SO24 9JH, U.K.
Tel: +44 (0)1962 735573   Fax: +44 (0)1962 733637
E-mail: sales@pocketbook.co.uk
Website: www.pocketbook.co.uk

All rights reserved. No part of this publication may be reproduced, stored in a retrieval system or transmitted in any form, or by any means, electronic, mechanical, photocopying, recording or otherwise, without the prior permission of the publishers.

This edition published 2009.

© John Sponton & Stewart Wright 2009.

British Library Cataloguing-in-Publication Data – A catalogue record for this book is available from the British Library.

ISBN 978 1 906610 05 0

Design, typesetting and graphics by **efex ltd**. Printed in U.K.

# CONTENTS

**INTRODUCTION** 5
What is an assessment centre?, applications, benefits, necessary elements

**WHAT YOU ARE MEASURING** 13
Building a role profile, benefits of working with competencies, when in the recruitment process, legal matters

**HOW YOU WILL MEASURE IT** 25
Types of assessment exercises with pros and cons, making exercise choices, using an exercise matrix, off-the-shelf or tailored exercises?, potential suppliers, designing your own exercises

**WHO MEASURES IT** 49
Choosing & sourcing assessors, training, ORCE technique: observing, recording, classifying & evaluating behaviour, defining acceptable

**ADVANCE PLANNING** 69
The role of the organiser, getting started, setting timescales, timetables, venue choice & specification, preparing & briefing candidates, final preparation

**ON THE DAY** 83
Before candidates arrive, when the assessors arrive, when the candidates arrive, briefing the candidates before, during & after the assessment centre

**WASH-UP & FEEDBACK** 91
Importance of the review session, setting rules & standards, completing the matrix, exploring the results, capturing discussions, communicating results, effective feedback

**REVIEWING THE PROCESS** 101
What to look for, capturing feedback from candidates & assessors, capturing exercise ratings, collating & monitoring results, comparing results to outcomes, development centres

## AUTHORS' INTRODUCTION

# WHO SHOULD READ THIS BOOK?

Assessment centres are increasingly being used for recruitment in the public and private sectors. They require a big commitment of time and effort to run properly – but they produce many direct and indirect benefits associated with more accurate, more objective and fairer recruitment.

This book is for anyone involved in or interested in assessment centres. This includes both HR and line managers and whether their involvement arises from being an organiser or an assessor. It will help you to understand:

- What assessment centres are
- The benefits they bring
- How they fit into a selection process
- How to plan them, design them and run them
- How to review them for effectiveness and value for money

By making this pocketbook your companion through your assessment centre design and implementation process, you will benefit from many useful hints and tips and avoid some common pitfalls.

Good luck with your assessment centre project! **John and Stewart.**

# INTRODUCTION

## INTRODUCTION

# WHAT IS AN ASSESSMENT CENTRE?

An assessment centre is an approach to selection in which multiple assessment methods and multiple assessors are used. Instead of attending a single interview, candidates undergo a range of different exercises or assessments designed to provide evidence of their performance in a range of relevant competencies.

In the 1950s, the American company AT&T was a pioneer in the use of this sort of technique for recruitment. The company used a special building called 'The Assessment Centre' in which to run its events. Since then the term assessment centre has become widely used to describe selection events based upon multiple exercises and multiple assessors.

# INTRODUCTION

## APPLICATIONS

Assessment centres can be used for:

- **Recruitment** – assessing a short-list of candidates who have applied for a role, whether internal candidates, external or a combination of the two
- **Restructuring** – assessing existing job holders for their suitability for existing roles or for re-designed roles, often necessary when an organisation restructures
- **Promotion** – assessing candidates against the skill-set for a role which represents a step-up for the appointed candidate

Then there are development centres which share certain characteristics with assessment centres. Development centres are used to assess individuals against a particular set of skills and then to plan their development with the help of the information gathered. The focus of this pocketbook is on assessment centres as an approach to selection. However, a summary of the key differences between assessment and development centres is shown on pages 108 and 109.

## INTRODUCTION

# KEY BENEFITS FOR THE ORGANISATION

There is no avoiding the fact that assessment centres are costly to design and run and, as with so many business tools, can be time-consuming to do properly. So what are the benefits?

- Research has shown that a well-designed, well-managed assessment centre is one of the fairest, most accurate and objective ways to predict the likelihood of someone's success in a role (source: M Smith, UMIST) – more so than just using, for example, an interview on its own or having to depend upon a candidate's paper qualifications

- Assessment centres can last typically from half a day to two days, requiring a considerable commitment from candidates. Less committed candidates will tend to select themselves out of the frame, saving time later for the organisation

## INTRODUCTION

# KEY BENEFITS FOR THE ORGANISATION

- Assessment centres provide an ideal means to consider external candidates alongside internal candidates in an objective way
- Different assessors, whether external consultants or HR and line managers trained in observation techniques, observe the candidates across different exercises, further increasing objectivity and accuracy
- A well-run assessment centre sends a positive message to the candidates about the organisation's commitment to its key resource – people

## INTRODUCTION

# KEY BENEFITS FOR LINE MANAGERS

- Ask any line manager about their recruitment experiences and you are likely to hear, 'He/she was very impressive at interview, but hasn't really lived up to expectations'. Assessment centres reduce that dependence upon interviews and relying on what a candidate **tells** you they can do – instead, you observe them in action and see how they **actually** behave

- Candidates experience a realistic taste of the work, through exercises which 'simulate' specific parts of the job, and are judged against the criteria important to that job, so there is less chance of unrealistic expectations if and when they are taken on

- You see them working across a range of contexts and situations, for example in a group – this is not possible through an interview alone

- A candidate with good interview techniques – but not much else – will not be able to sustain their performance through the extended nature of an assessment centre

- Line managers who act as assessors will find the skill set invaluable when back in the day job and will develop as individuals too

INTRODUCTION

# KEY BENEFITS FOR CANDIDATES

- Candidates are given a range of opportunities to demonstrate their skills, rather than having to depend on just their interview performance
- They can be given realistic exercises which can help them to understand the demands of the job better – this is particularly helpful for graduate or apprentice recruitment
- They can 'see' the organisation in action; for example, by having tours, seeing presentations and meeting line managers or previous successful recruits at specific points in the assessment centre timetable
- They will benefit from receiving powerful feedback about their performance

## INTRODUCTION

# NECESSARY ELEMENTS

A good assessment centre is only as good as the quality of its parts, all of which are bound together:

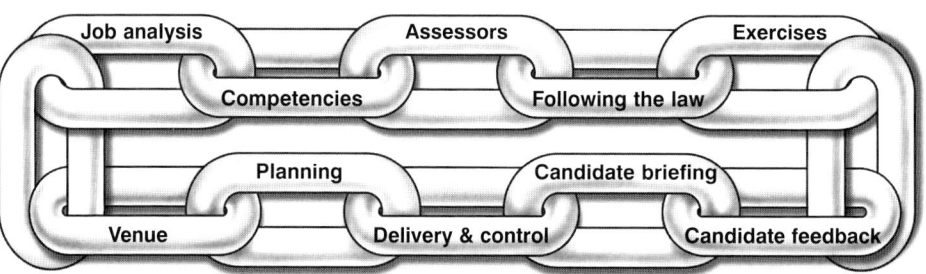

All of these themes will be explored in this book.

# What you are measuring

## WHAT YOU ARE MEASURING

# BUILDING A ROLE PROFILE

When designing an assessment centre, the first critical step is to ensure that you know what you want to measure.

Start with the job description, which should provide you with the job's purpose (why the role exists) and a summary of the tasks and responsibilities associated with the role. Next, you need to look at (or create) the person specification, which builds upon the picture of the job tasks and responsibilities, and distinguishes between personal attributes essential for success in the role *(must have qualities)* and those that are desirable *(nice to have)*. Attributes can include: experience, qualifications held, knowledge and skills or competencies.

In a wider recruitment process, **attributes** such as experience, knowledge and qualifications are normally measured early in the process. Assessment centres tend to focus on measuring skills or **competencies**.

## WHAT YOU ARE MEASURING

# WORKING WITH COMPETENCIES

Competencies describe particular behaviours or abilities. They are written in a way to help managers assess individuals for either recruitment or development purposes. As an example, here is a competency for team working:

- Gives help and active support to colleagues
- Does their fair share of work
- Takes on work willingly
- Tries their hand at different tasks to benefit the team

Competency definitions will vary from organisation to organisation, but there are also a number of generic competency frameworks published by organisations such as psychometric test publishers.

Organisations may also choose to write their own competency definitions specific to a role (or band of role). For example, the competency of team working could be defined at three levels: administrative, professional and managerial.

## WHAT YOU ARE MEASURING

# COMMONLY USED COMPETENCIES

Common competencies include:

- Analysis and problem solving
- Decision making
- Planning and organising
- Creativity
- Flexibility
- Persuasive communication
- Team working
- Leadership
- Self-motivation and resilience
- Commercial awareness
- Strategic thinking

## WHAT YOU ARE MEASURING

# BENEFITS OF COMPETENCIES

The benefits of using competencies in an assessment centre are that they:

- Provide a clear focus for each assessor as to what they are seeking to measure in each exercise
- Provide a common language for all assessors to use
- Are described in observable terms and are therefore easier to measure in an assessment centre setting

It is useful to prioritise the most important six to eight competencies for effective performance in a role and have these as the foundation for the design of your assessment centre.

WHAT YOU ARE MEASURING

# WHEN IN THE RECRUITMENT PROCESS

A recruitment process is often likened to a series of filters. You start with a number of candidates who are then screened/assessed against relevant criteria and competencies. It is best to run an assessment centre at the final stage of a recruitment process.

Your early stage selection processes will be about making broad-brush distinctions – do we invite to the next stage or not? As you move through the filters, you are dealing with fewer candidates (of a higher overall quality) and will also be measuring competencies that require more sophisticated tools to assess.

Assessment centres have been shown to be one of the most accurate forms of selection. It is at the final stage that you will need this better quality selection method to help differentiate between the remaining higher-quality candidates.

Assessment centres are also one of the more expensive forms of selection and using them sooner in a recruitment process will be less appropriate on cost grounds.

## WHAT YOU ARE MEASURING

# DIRECT & INDIRECT DISCRIMINATION

As you develop your job description, person specification and competencies, it is vital that your criteria and processes stay within the law. This will ensure that you are being fair as well as effective with your assessment. Two important concepts underpin recruitment legislation – **direct discrimination**, and **indirect discrimination**. Both are **illegal** in the UK unless the employer can prove genuine and justifiable occupational requirement.

**Direct discrimination** *is treating a person, or a group, less favourably than others.* Examples of direct discrimination: not offering a job to a man because of his gender; or refusing to offer a job to a candidate because he/she is from a particular racial group.

**Indirect discrimination** *is applying a condition which certain groups are less likely to be able to meet.* An example would be specifying that 'candidates need to be over 1.7m tall', when their height will make no difference to their ability to do the job effectively. Women as a group are proportionately less likely to be over 1.7m than men. So if you cannot justify why candidates need to be over 1.7m tall, this is indirect discrimination.

## WHAT YOU ARE MEASURING

# CURRENT LEGISLATION

The following legislation makes direct and indirect discrimination unlawful in the relevant area:

- Sex Discrimination Act (1975)
- Race Relations Act (1976)
- Disability Discrimination Act (1995)
- Employment Equality (Sexual Orientation) Regulations (2003)
- Employment Equality (Religion and Belief) Regulations (2003)
- Employment Equality (Age) Regulations (2006)

## WHAT YOU ARE MEASURING

# APPLYING CONDITIONS

Applying a condition which results in direct or indirect discrimination is unlawful unless the condition can be **justified**. For example, a person who works in a warehouse might need to lift heavy weights as an essential part of the job. The job and person specification would reinforce the justification of this requirement.

Certain groups – but only a few – are exempt from the relevant legislation on the grounds of safety or decency; for example, public lavatory attendants. Also some organisations are allowed to show discrimination when recruiting if it is important to the nature of their business. A Chinese restaurant, for example, may feel it needs to recruit Chinese waiters.

If an assessment decision is challenged, the onus rests on the employer to justify why that person was not appointed.

## WHAT YOU ARE MEASURING

# DISABILITY

Specific to the Disability Discrimination Act, you need to make any **reasonable adjustments** in your assessment processes to ensure that a disabled person is not at a disadvantage. For example, when inviting a candidate with special requirements to an assessment centre:

- Ask the candidate in advance what steps can be taken to help that person give of their best
- What exactly is their condition(s)?
- What steps have been taken historically to assist the candidate with similar processes, or when in the workplace, or when sitting exams?

## WHAT YOU ARE MEASURING
# DISABILITY

Explain the assessment process in more detail to the candidate. Ask them what support they would find useful:

- Make the necessary arrangements and check these with the candidate in advance of the assessment centre

- Finally, make sure the necessary arrangements happen in practice and all assessors fully understand what additional support needs to happen and when

## WHAT YOU ARE MEASURING

# DATA PROTECTION

Other key legislation in the UK includes the **Data Protection Act**. Individuals have a right of access, upon request, to any information relating to them (either stored on paper or electronically). The act covers the collection, holding, use and destruction of the data.

To stay within the spirit of the legislation:

- Ensure your assessment criteria relate to the areas covered on your job description and person specification and ensure that these are relevant and justifiable

- Keep full and relevant records (including any interview and assessment paperwork), but do not keep these for longer than is justifiable or reasonable

Most employers would hold recruitment and assessment information for 12 months; if a candidate is appointed, then the papers can become part of the individual's personnel file. For further information, contact the Data Protection Registrar on 01625 545475.

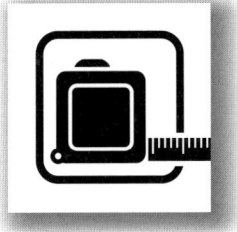

# How you will measure it

## HOW YOU WILL MEASURE IT

# ABILITY TESTS

We now look at some of the more widely used types of assessment exercises and where they might best be used. The key role of the assessors is covered in the next chapter.

Once you know the competencies you want to measure, there is a wide range of exercises that you can draw upon to gather information. Bespoke exercises can be designed specific to your organisation – more about this later – or you can purchase off-the-shelf from an exercise publisher.

We start with psychometric tests. These are carefully researched, standardised exercises in which candidates' results are compared to large, relevant sample groups. Tests can look at a wide range of specific abilities, important to explore for many roles – from senior management through to administrative positions. (For more detail on this subject, see The Psychometric Testing Pocketbook.)

Two key areas for a significant number of professional and management roles are **verbal and numerical reasoning skills.** These tests look at the ability to evaluate the logic of various kinds of argument; and the ability to make quick and accurate inferences from information presented in a numerical format.

# HOW YOU WILL MEASURE IT

## ABILITY TESTS

**Ideal for measuring:**
Analysis and problem solving, but largely limited to this or similar competencies.

 **Watch out for:**

- To use the best quality tests, you will need to be trained and have authorised access to the materials. This can be a costly and time-consuming process. Depending upon the volume of need, consider using a trained external consultant who can also give best advice on their use

- It can be easy to place too much emphasis upon low or high test scores. When planning your assessment centre, be clear and realistic about what you are using the tests to measure and the standard you expect a candidate to achieve

## HOW YOU WILL MEASURE IT

# PERSONALITY QUESTIONNAIRES

Personality questionnaires are structured forms of self-assessment that explore how candidates see themselves in terms of their typical approach to different tasks and situations. They are designed to provide an insight into how candidates behave at work, in respect of the way they relate to others, the way they approach and solve problems, and their feelings and emotions (anxiety levels etc).

Personality questionnaires do this by measuring candidates' preferences against large sample groups. They are untimed and, unlike ability tests, do not have right and wrong answers. They tend to be used more in managerial and professional assessments but can be used with any employment group.

## HOW YOU WILL MEASURE IT

# PERSONALITY QUESTIONNAIRES

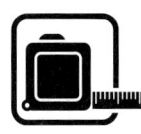

**Ideal for measuring:**
The majority of competencies, but remember that you are only getting the candidate's self-assessment perspective.

 **Watch out for:**

- Be careful how much weight you place upon the candidate's self-assessment perspective when reviewing the results – make sure you have evidence from other types of exercises available in your assessment centre process to bring a balanced picture

- You will need to be trained in the product concerned and have authorised access to the materials. Depending upon the volume of need, it may make more sense to use a trained external consultant

## HOW YOU WILL MEASURE IT

# GROUP DISCUSSION EXERCISES

In group discussion exercises, candidates working as part of a team undertake a practical task or are asked to solve a series of business problems under timed conditions.

The situations are often fictitious. Candidates might, for example, be presented with some management/staff issues to tackle, or be told that the company is considering office relocation options and given data on two or more sites to consider. The scenarios are deliberately not clear-cut so that debate and discussion can ensue.

In some situations, candidates will be assigned a particular role, representing a particular functional or business area. In other situations, all candidates will be presented with the same remit. Depending on the nature of the exercise, candidates may have preparation time at the start of the exercise to review background documentation.

During the exercise, assessors observe how candidates interact with others and how they approach the problems in question.

## HOW YOU WILL MEASURE IT

# GROUP DISCUSSION EXERCISES

### Ideal for measuring:
Competencies associated with leading others, communicating, persuading/influencing others, decision making, team working, planning and organising.

 **Watch out for:**

- Some candidates can seek to dominate or project a particular style in group discussions. Consider how quieter candidates can be encouraged to contribute, for example, by asking each of them to chair part of the discussion

- A lot of assessor resource is required to run and observe group exercises and assessors need to be properly trained. Each assessor should observe no more than two candidates! Consider the impact of this in your timetable and assessor training design

## HOW YOU WILL MEASURE IT

# ANALYSIS EXERCISES

Analysis exercises present the candidate with a large amount of information relating to a particular work scenario.

One example is the 'in-tray' (or in-basket) exercise format. Here candidates are often asked to step in for a colleague, or take on a new role at short notice, and respond to various letters, memos and emails covering a variety of issues or problems to be tackled.

Another example is the case study format where candidates are asked to analyse a wide range of business information and to produce a report (and/or presentation) with specific recommendations.

## HOW YOU WILL MEASURE IT

# ANALYSIS EXERCISES

### Ideal for measuring:
Competencies associated with analysis and problem solving, decision making, commercial awareness, planning and organising (depending upon the topic).

 **Watch out for:**

➤ These sorts of exercises are particularly good at bringing to life what a candidate would actually do when dealing with a particular problem. However, they can be complex to design and score if they are to provide accurate and consistent results. Consider the benefits of buying in off-the-shelf exercises and consultants specifically experienced in their use

➤ Because of their complexity, they can be time-consuming to administer as well – often up to two hours. Consider the impact of this when designing your timetable

➤ An off-the-shelf analysis exercise could take an experienced assessor anything from 30 minutes to 75 minutes to score

## HOW YOU WILL MEASURE IT

## PRESENTATION EXERCISES

Candidates are asked to make a presentation. This can be on a topic unrelated to work or may replicate the type of real life scenario that they could come across if successful in their application.

Traditionally, the topic is given to the candidates before they attend the assessment centre so that they have time to prepare.

## HOW YOU WILL MEASURE IT

# PRESENTATION EXERCISES

**Ideal for measuring:**
Technical skills (depending upon the topic); and competencies associated with communication, persuasion, influencing, planning and organising.

 **Watch out for:**

- Candidates can over-prepare or indeed draw upon others' help in their preparation if given the topic in advance. You could give the topic to the candidates on the day, but you will need to decide whether they have enough preparation time to do it justice. If so, every candidate must then be given identical periods of preparation time in the timetable

- For some more technical or back-office roles, presentation skills may not be particularly important; in this case, use a presentation exercise with care, and focus your assessment more on the content of the presentation than on the skill of the delivery

## HOW YOU WILL MEASURE IT

# ROLE-PLAY EXERCISES

Role-play exercises are designed to provide a simulation of an important aspect of the role. Depending on the nature of the role, the exercise could take place over the phone or could be face-to-face. The phone context can be real (the role-player is in a separate room connected via an internal telephone link) or simulated (the role-player and candidate sit back-to-back and hold a conversation without eye contact as if over the telephone).

Role-play exercises will create a particular scenario and will provide candidates with certain tasks or outcomes that need to be achieved. Scenarios could include: a sales meeting; performance review; training course delivery; disciplinary meeting; or customer complaint handling. Candidates take the exercise and are assessed individually. Ideally, an assessor observes the candidate while a second individual in the assessment team acts as the role-player.

## HOW YOU WILL MEASURE IT

# ROLE-PLAY EXERCISES

**Ideal for measuring:**
Management-related competencies; interpersonal-related competencies; and competencies associated with problem solving and decision making. Role-play exercises are widely used in the assessment of customer-facing roles.

### Watch out for:

- The role-player can be one of the assessors but it is critically important that she or he can consistently and objectively play the same role for all of the candidates. Consider the benefits of using external consultants or even professional actors to play these parts, although this will increase costs

- Inevitably some candidates will still struggle with the simulated nature of the exercise, however well it is designed

## HOW YOU WILL MEASURE IT

# STRUCTURED COMPETENCY INTERVIEWS

Structured competency interviews are designed to gather specific information by asking for examples of situations when candidates have demonstrated particular skills/competencies, or how they have approached particular problems.

An example of a structured competency interview question exploring the area of planning and organising could be: *'Give me an example of a recent project you were responsible for planning'*.

Follow-up questions by the interviewer would then be used to explore the responses in further detail.

This structured approach has been shown to be far more accurate than more traditional forms of interview-based assessment.

## HOW YOU WILL MEASURE IT

# STRUCTURED COMPETENCY INTERVIEWS

**Ideal for measuring:**
A very wide range of competencies.

### Watch out for:

- Although a very acceptable form of assessment to both line managers and candidates alike, remember that the quality of assessment derived from an interview is only as good as the quality of the interviewers, their questions and the candidate's interview technique. Some other candidates would do a good job if appointed but lack interview technique, so do not place an inappropriate emphasis on their communication skills

- Use structured interview guides which provide targeted questions and suggested 'probes' (follow-up questions) against the chosen competencies for the interviewers

- Ensure that your other exercises **test out** the candidates in the selected competencies. Do not depend upon them just saying they are good at something; see it in practice!

## HOW YOU WILL MEASURE IT

## MAKING EXERCISE CHOICES

When choosing exercises, you should consider:

- The competencies to be assessed – using the previous pages as a guide, which exercises will provide the best opportunities for candidates to display their capability in the top six to eight competencies that you have chosen for your assessment centre?

- The context of the role and the working situation in which the competency should be displayed. For example, if the actual job requires a candidate to persuade on a one-to-one basis, as well as in a group, make sure you have both one-to-one and group exercises, so that the competency of persuasive communication can be appropriately assessed

- The exercise level – do the exercises measure the competencies at an appropriate level? Exercise publishers classify their exercises as being suitable for different levels of roles including: non-management; graduate; first line management; middle management, and senior management. Details of a number of exercise publishers are on page 45

# HOW YOU WILL MEASURE IT

## USING AN EXERCISE MATRIX

Developing an exercise matrix is a good way to choose which exercises to consider. The matrix is used to chart the relationship between your competencies and how you intend to measure them by the different exercises. The example below shows the relationship between six competencies and how they could be measured:

| Competencies | Verbal & numerical reasoning tests | Personality questionnaire | Group discussion | In-tray exercise | Structured competency interview |
|---|---|---|---|---|---|
| Analysis and problem solving | ✔✔ | ✔ | | ✔✔ | |
| Commercial awareness | | | ✔✔ | ✔✔ | ✔✔ |
| Decision making | | ✔ | ✔✔ | ✔✔ | |
| Team working | | ✔ | ✔✔ | | ✔✔ |
| Planning and organising | | ✔ | | ✔✔ | ✔✔ |
| Persuasive communication | | ✔ | ✔✔ | | ✔✔ |

**Key:** ✔✔ Primary source of evidence   ✔ Secondary source of evidence

## HOW YOU WILL MEASURE IT

# DEVELOPING AN EXERCISE MATRIX

In developing the matrix:

- Use at least two different exercises to measure any one competency

- Differentiate between exercises that offer 'primary' evidence (or good opportunity) for measurement of the competency versus those that offer 'secondary' evidence (less opportunity for the evidence to be observed)

- Personality questionnaires are often classed as secondary sources, as they are based on how the candidates see themselves

- Avoid measuring any more than five competency areas by any one observed exercise – research suggests that the more competencies you try to measure, the less well they are measured

- Consider if any competencies have emerged as more important than others in the job analysis process. When reviewing results after the assessment centre, you could then attach more weight to these scores

## HOW YOU WILL MEASURE IT

# OFF-THE-SHELF OR TAILORED EXERCISES?

In considering which exercises to use, you also need to consider the relative merits of off-the-shelf exercises, which can be purchased from specialist suppliers, versus tailored exercises.

**Advantages of off-the-shelf exercises:**
- ✔ Immediately available
- ✔ Cheaper for smaller volumes of usage
- ✔ Well developed and tested

**Disadvantages of off-the-shelf exercises:**
- ✘ Candidates may have encountered them before and developed familiarity
- ✘ Not tailored to your specific competencies
- ✘ Less likely directly to reflect the role and organisation
- ✘ You may need to satisfy the exercise publisher about your assessment expertise before they will allow you to use the exercise. Specific training may be required – this of course maintains quality but does add to the time and cost involved

## HOW YOU WILL MEASURE IT

# OFF-THE-SHELF OR TAILORED EXERCISES?

**Advantages of tailored exercises:**
- ✔ Can accurately reflect the role and culture of an organisation
- ✔ Designed around your specific competencies
- ✔ No ongoing running costs once developed
- ✔ Restricted circulation – the exercise will only be used by you

**Disadvantages of tailored exercises:**
- ✘ Will require time and cost to design and develop
- ✘ Will need to be regularly updated and reviewed

## HOW YOU WILL MEASURE IT

## POTENTIAL SUPPLIERS

The following firms have strong reputations for psychometric and/or assessment centre exercises and will make a good starting point from which to explore the availability and suitability of exercises:

- Assessment & Development Consultants: www.adc.uk.com
- Hogrefe: www.hogrefe.co.uk
- OPP®: www.opp.eu.com
- Previsor (formerly ASE): www.previsor.co.uk
- SHL Group: www.shl.com

Another option is to customise an existing off-the-shelf product, provided that you have clear permission from the relevant exercise publisher beforehand. This could include adding a presentation element into a written analysis exercise or adjusting the timings in a particular exercise to reflect more accurately the demands of a particular role.

## HOW YOU WILL MEASURE IT

# DESIGNING YOUR OWN EXERCISES

## BEFORE YOU START

If you decide to design your own exercise(s):

- Be clear in your mind that you have the time to invest in designing the exercise, and that others will give you their time in trialling and commenting upon it

- Know what competencies you want to measure

- Consider the level of the role and the required difficulty pitch of the exercise

- You will already have given thought to what contexts or situations you want to see reflected in your choice of exercises. You now need to take this a stage further and think about the most appropriate type of exercise to design, and to 'flesh out' the situations that can be used in your self-designed exercise

- To help you, gather information from others – what sort of situations and examples could be used? How can these be made anonymous in the exercise? Involve people who know the role well (such as HR, existing line managers or people who have performed the role before)

## HOW YOU WILL MEASURE IT

# DESIGNING YOUR OWN EXERCISES
## DRAFTING THE EXERCISE

- When drafting the exercise, avoid jargon and be attuned to the backgrounds of the candidates (whether they are likely to be external candidates, or new to your sector, etc)

- Draft the appropriate scoring guides too – be as specific as you can about the performance and behaviour you would expect a strong and a weak candidate to show, and incorporate actual examples in your scoring guides

- Show the draft to people who know the job well and get their feedback

HOW YOU WILL MEASURE IT

# DESIGNING YOUR OWN EXERCISES
## TRIALLING & AMENDING

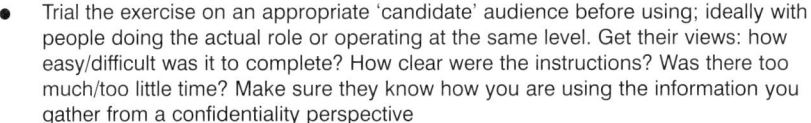

- Trial the exercise on an appropriate 'candidate' audience before using; ideally with people doing the actual role or operating at the same level. Get their views: how easy/difficult was it to complete? How clear were the instructions? Was there too much/too little time? Make sure they know how you are using the information you gather from a confidentiality perspective

- Ask the person who administered the trial exercise for their views as well – how clear were the instructions for them? Do they have any suggested changes?

- Ask someone to score the trial responses – how easy to use were the scoring guidelines? Remember that real candidates will be under more pressure and rarely score as well as the guinea pigs!

# WHO MEASURES IT

## WHO MEASURES IT

# CHOOSING THE ASSESSORS

Good assessors are critical to the success of the assessment centre. Choosing the right assessors is a bit like selecting the right candidate for a job! It is the responsibility of the event organiser to ensure that they are of a suitable standard.

**Good assessors need to be:**
- Objective
- Observant
- Knowledgeable about the process and the exercises
- Trained
- Qualified, if using certain psychometric products
- Thorough
- Reliable

If you have an available pool of assessors who meet all of these criteria, seek to represent as diverse a range of backgrounds and profiles as possible in relation to factors such as gender, age, ethnicity, etc when pulling together your assessor team.

## WHO MEASURES IT

# SOURCING THE ASSESSORS

Your assessors could be drawn from HR or relevant line managers or other stakeholders.

Having a mix of assessors – albeit sharing the qualities noted previously – helps to bring a range of objective perspectives to the assessment process.

**Line managers and/or stakeholders/service users as assessors:**
- ✔ Involving line managers will increase their buy-in to the process
- ✔ They will bring their understanding of the roles to the assessment process
- ✔ It gives them development opportunities as well as involvement
- ✔ They have appropriate knowledge about the organisation, the role and the team which can be shared with candidates, either formally (eg through a presentation to candidates) or informally (eg in scheduled break times)

> Ensure that your assessors have the right attitude towards objective assessment and are willing to invest the time to make the process work properly.

## WHO MEASURES IT

## SOURCING THE ASSESSORS

**External consultants as assessors:**

- ✔ Involving them will show the candidates that the organisation is particularly committed to independent assessment
- ✔ They can bring specialist knowledge and expertise in certain assessment products such as psychometrics
- ✔ They should need less or indeed no time spent on training

### Watch out for:

- ➤ There will be direct cost implications
- ➤ Depending upon their familiarity with the organisation, they may have limited knowledge of its day-to-day business and how it works. This may make them in turn less well placed to answer candidates' questions, but it will not necessarily affect their abilities as assessors

## WHO MEASURES IT

# TRAINING THE ASSESSORS

Once you have selected the assessors, it is essential to ensure, **before** the assessment centre runs, that they are very familiar with:

- Running the exercises properly
- Scoring the exercises objectively
- The timetable
- Legal issues and responsibilities

Consider using the training services of one of the assessment suppliers listed on page 45, drawing upon their specialist expertise in this area.

## WHO MEASURES IT

# TRAINING THE ASSESSORS

Whether you run the training yourself, use an external supplier, or opt for a combination of the two, the training could last from half a day to three days' duration, depending upon the assessors' level of involvement with the exercises (for example, acting as administrators only or as administrators and scorers) and the number of exercises to be covered. The training should cover:

- Building familiarity with the competencies to be used
- Walking through the timetable
- The wider assessment process – what is happening before and after the assessment centre
- Clarifying assessors' roles
- Appreciating the candidates' perspectives – assessors should sit some of the exercises in the safe setting of the training course!

## WHO MEASURES IT

# TRAINING THE ASSESSORS (CONT'D)

- Practice in administering the exercises
- Practice in scoring the exercises using the ORCE model (see next page) as appropriate
- Legal responsibilities
- What to expect in the review or wash-up session
- How candidate feedback will be handled

> ⚠️ If you plan to run the assessor training yourself, ensure that you do not exceed the terms of any licensing agreements with test publishers' materials which you might share with participants or reproduce.

## WHO MEASURES IT

# OBSERVE, RECORD, CLASSIFY & EVALUATE BEHAVIOUR

Assessors need to be competent in accurately measuring the competencies displayed by the candidates during the group, presentation and role-play exercises. They must therefore be trained to capture and measure this information accurately.

A widely used approach for doing this is called the ORCE model: Observe, Record, Classify and Evaluate. This model is also used during the structured interview process.

WHO MEASURES IT

# ORCE IN A NUTSHELL

**O** bserve – while the exercise is happening, assessors continuously observe what is being said and done by the candidates

**R** ecord – while the exercise is happening, assessors record as fully as they can what is being said and done by the candidates. Given the time and concentration required to do both of these, assessors should observe no more than two candidates at once – and ideally observe just one if they are new to the process

**C** lassify – immediately after the exercise has finished, assessors review their notes and decide which competencies their evidence relates to

**E** valuate – after the evidence has been classified, assessors weigh up the evidence and award ratings against the competencies

## WHO MEASURES IT

# ORCE IN A NUTSHELL

The ORCE model helps assessors to be as objective and accurate as they can be with their decision-making process.

- Assessors use one of the assessor observation forms (shown on the following pages) depending on whether they are observing one or two candidates

- They 'track' their candidates' performance during the exercise by using the ORCE model – observing and recording their observations during the exercise, followed by classifying and evaluating immediately after the exercise finishes

A summary of each stage is shown on pages 61-67.

# WHO MEASURES IT

## ASSESSOR OBSERVATION FORM

Candidate: _____  Assessor: _____

Exercise: _____  Date: _____

| Time | Record on candidate | Comment |
|------|---------------------|---------|
|      |                     |         |

# WHO MEASURES IT

## ASSESSOR OBSERVATION FORM

Candidate A: _____  Assessor: _____

Candidate B: _____  Exercise: _____  Date: _____

| Time | Record on candidate A | Comment | Record on candidate B |
|------|----------------------|---------|----------------------|
|      |                      |         |                      |

# WHO MEASURES IT
## OBSERVING BEHAVIOUR

- You are seeking to capture non-judgmental observations of the candidates during the exercise

- Essentially, what you are doing at this stage is acting like a video camera – recording facts free from any interpretations (interpretation will happen later in the process)

## WHO MEASURES IT

# **R**ECORDING BEHAVIOUR

- Record as much factual evidence as possible on what you saw and what you heard
- Write verbatim quotes wherever possible
- Record non-verbal behaviour in your notes, but do so objectively
- If you need to summarise, write key words/abbreviations so you can expand upon your notes later
- Note the time at regular intervals, especially if observing a candidate(s) who contributes less

Taking notes in the above manner is essential to ensure that subsequent stages are based on an accurate picture of what happened.

## WHO MEASURES IT

# **C**LASSIFYING BEHAVIOUR

- Do it as soon as the exercise finishes and the candidate(s) have left the room

- Review each piece of evidence recorded in your notes. This could be what you saw the candidate do, or heard them say, or how they said it

- Relate the evidence to the competencies that you are looking to measure in the exercise (as shown in the matrix, see page 41). Annotate your notes, indicating if the behaviour is positive or negative. For example, *PC(+)* means positive evidence of *Persuasive Communication*

- It is helpful to use a different colour of pen for the annotation

- Remember that some of the evidence you noted may relate to more than one competency

- Omission of behaviour could also be important (negative) evidence, such as a candidate who does not respond to a direct question they were asked

## WHO MEASURES IT

# CLASSIFYING BEHAVIOUR

Here is a sample extract from a completed assessor observation form.

It shows the assessor's notes and classification for an extract of the candidate's behaviour derived from an around-the-table group exercise.

It shows the abbreviated classifications awarded for Persuasive Communication (negative in this instance), Relating to Others (negative in this instance) and Planning & Organising (positive in this instance).

This process would be repeated for all of the candidate's behaviour observed in the exercise.

## WHO MEASURES IT

# **C**LASSIFYING BEHAVIOUR

As you can see from the extract below, this assessor has reviewed her abbreviated notes which were recorded during the exercise. Immediately after the exercise, she applied the classification as shown in the 'Comment' column.

Candidate: Sharon Smith  
Assessor: Nuz Shah  
Exercise: Group ex  
Date: dd/mm/yy

| Time | Record on candidate | Comment |
|---|---|---|
| 3 mins | (looks at Bill, unsmiling, taps pen on table, points at Bill) | PC –   RTO – |
|  | I think you are wrong….. that would not work (pause). |  |
|  | Instead – we need to set a clear plan……. anyone done anything like this before? Let's give 5 minutes to set some goals………. | P&O + |

## WHO MEASURES IT
# EVALUATING BEHAVIOUR

Guard against your own biases or subjective opinions when evaluating assessment performance. Weigh up both the quality and the quantity of evidence you have gathered in each of the competency areas based upon the evidence recorded. Use a rating scale such as the one shown opposite.

Ideally, assessors involved in group exercises should discuss their findings before the main review session. This enables scores to be fine-tuned and calibrated. This is particularly relevant for scoring group exercises where individual candidates' behaviour needs to be seen in the context of what other candidates did or said at the time.

## WHO MEASURES IT

# EVALUATING BEHAVIOUR

| Rating | Description |
|---|---|
| **5** Exceptional | Meets all or virtually all of the competency description – no significant omissions |
| **4** Good | Meets most of the description; many indicators observed in full and others partially; any omissions or negative areas were not critical to the overall performance in this area |
| **3** Acceptable | Meets more than half of the description – is capable of performing at the level required; some negative evidence observed |
| **2** Some weakness | Meets less than half of competency description; some critical positive indicators omitted; more negative areas/evidence observed |
| **1** Poor | Meets almost none of the competency definition; very little positive evidence observed; negative indicators are dominant |

## WHO MEASURES IT

# DEFINING 'ACCEPTABLE' AS A RATING

Assuming that you are using this five-point rating scale, it is important to acknowledge that, by awarding a rating of '3', you are stating that you have observed evidence to suggest that the candidate is capable of performing to the required, or acceptable level, in this particular competency.

> ⚠ It is vital that this benchmark is applied consistently to all candidates by all assessors.

# ADVANCE PLANNING

## ADVANCE PLANNING

# THE ROLE OF THE ORGANISER

As the organiser, your role will be critical to the success of the assessment centre.

The organiser's role is a large one – planning the event and ensuring it runs smoothly on the day.

An important consideration for the organiser is whether to appoint a separate individual to act as an event administrator at the assessment centre. The event administrator can meet and greet candidates, circulate appropriate paperwork to candidates/assessors and then collect and collate completed paperwork.

The organiser can also be an assessor, and/or act as an event administrator. However, the organiser should be careful not to overburden him or herself with assessment duties, and so allow sufficient time to undertake the management role.

ADVANCE PLANNING

# GETTING STARTED

As the organiser of the assessment centre, leave nothing to C-H-A-N-C-E:

**C**andidates – have been told where the assessment centre is running, what it will consist of, what they need to do beforehand and what to bring with them.

**H**andouts and paperwork – all documents have been designed, checked and printed off ready for the day.

**A**ssessors – have been trained in the Observe, Record, Classify and Evaluate (ORCE) process, are familiar with any exercises in which they are involved, clear about their roles and legal responsibilities and know where they need to be and when.

**N**asty surprises – you are prepared for worst-case scenarios.

**C**atering and venue – break times and meals are fully catered for, the venue has been booked and rooms checked for suitability.

**E**quipment – external materials and/or equipment have been ordered and are ready for use.

ADVANCE PLANNING

# SETTING TIMESCALES

As the organiser, you also need to plan:

- When does the assessment centre need to take place? Remember that availability of assessors, as well as venue, will be a factor
- When and how do assessors need to be booked and trained? Ideally their training should be carried out shortly before the first assessment centre takes place
- When and how will candidates be told that they are being invited to attend?
- How long will candidates need to complete any online assessment exercises prior to the event?
- When and how can candidates expect to receive news about the outcome and receive feedback on the results?

## ADVANCE PLANNING

# SETTING TIMESCALES

Top tips for the organiser:

- Make up a master plan which captures all the details (you could use project management software or a spreadsheet program) so that you are clear exactly what needs to happen and by when

- Make sure that your plan covers the requirements of candidates, assessors, exercise suppliers, the venue and any consultants who might be involved

- 'Walk through' your plan from the perspective of each of these groups to check that you have not missed anything

## ADVANCE PLANNING

# DRAFTING A GOOD TIMETABLE

A good assessment centre needs a good timetable which takes account of:

- How long each individual exercise needs to be introduced, administered and run and with which candidates and which assessors. Be particularly careful with allowing time for any open-ended or non-timed exercises such as certain psychometric exercises – err upon more generous estimated completion times

- How long each individual exercise needs for scoring

- What other events or activities need to take place, such as any presentations to the candidates

- Venue constraints such as the number and sizes of available rooms and equipment limitations

- Break times

## ADVANCE PLANNING

# TOP TIPS FOR A GOOD TIMETABLE

- Try to keep it simple; factor in some slippage time for unexpected events such as a candidate or an assessor running late
- Avoid group exercises first thing in the morning – allow the candidates a little time to relax in each other's company. The best time for a group exercise is late morning or just before or after lunch – the latter keeps up candidates' energy levels in the early afternoon!
- At the start of the day, include an overview of the day's schedule and (if appropriate) a company presentation. As well as sharing useful information, this helps candidates relax and allows them to get used to the venue and each other
- Make sure that the exercises which take longest to score, eg in-tray/analysis exercises, are given early on, to make full use of available assessor scoring time
- Psychometric exercises generally involve a single assessor to administer, and are good to use when candidates might otherwise be unoccupied
- Some 'break' periods during the timetable are acceptable but avoid prolonged periods of inactivity for candidates

## ADVANCE PLANNING

# CHECKING THE DRAFT TIMETABLE

Now test your draft timetable thoroughly. Make sure that it works from all the different perspectives:

- Candidates
- Assessors – they need time to review and classify their assessor observation forms and develop their evaluations. Also, after a group exercise, allow time for them to discuss their findings before the main review session, enabling scores to be fine-tuned and calibrated. This is particularly relevant for scoring group exercises, where an individual candidate's behaviour often needs to be seen in the context of what others did or said at the time
- Rooms
- Catering and break times

Make sure that no candidate is unduly advantaged or disadvantaged by the timetable – for example, any candidate planning time or 'waiting' time should be evenly distributed.

## ADVANCE PLANNING

# VENUE CHOICE

A well-designed assessment centre can easily be let down by poor venue facilities.
Firstly, weigh up the pros and cons of using in-house facilities against external facilities. Running the event in your organisation's premises may be cheaper but challenge yourself as to the suitability of these.

- How might these facilities appear to candidates?

- Will your assessors concentrate as much as they should at the assessment centre if work-based distractions are present?

## ADVANCE PLANNING

# VENUE SPECIFICATION

When choosing a venue, check that:

- The rooms to be used are suitable, particularly with regard to lighting, noise-proofing and technology facilities, and preferably are positioned close together
- Early access to the rooms can be gained on the day
- Public or shared waiting areas are suitable for use by the candidates
- It has been clearly agreed beforehand who is supplying any equipment – the venue organisers or you
- Any fire drill arrangements and alarm-testing times will cause minimal disruption
- The needs of any candidates with special requirements will be met

ADVANCE PLANNING

# PREPARING THE CANDIDATES

Even before short-listing takes place, candidates should be told about the need, if short-listed, to attend an assessment centre and about possible dates. Those who are subsequently short-listed need to be told the chosen date as soon as possible.

When communicating with candidates, imagine that they are all customers of your organisation. Make sure any information sent out is crystal-clear and of a high quality. Put yourself in their shoes and identify what information you would like to receive if you were a candidate, and how you would like to be treated.

The information and contact process with the candidate is an opportunity to present the organisation in a positive light – one that is committed to best practice in assessment.

## ADVANCE PLANNING

# BRIEFING THE CANDIDATES

As soon as you can, send the short-listed candidates information about the assessment centre. This should contain, as print-outs, attachments or micro-site links:

- A note of congratulations for reaching this stage
- Where and when they need to attend, with maps and accommodation arrangements if necessary
- The broad format of the assessment centre, descriptions of the exercises and how they can prepare
- Company information or background briefing
- The job and person specification
- Organisational policy on travel expense reimbursement to avoid misunderstandings at a later stage

## ADVANCE PLANNING

## BRIEFING THE CANDIDATES

You should also cover:

- Clear instructions on the means by which and the date by when they should confirm their attendance

- What they should bring – eg, examination proofs of achievement or copies of presentations

- What they should do beforehand – eg, whether any online assessment exercises need to be completed or presentations prepared for

- Dress code information

- Whom they should contact in the event of any special requirements which may require adjustments to the exercises, and how to do this

## ADVANCE PLANNING

# FINAL PREPARATION

A day or two before the assessment centre is due to take place, the organiser should:

- Confirm everyone's attendance at the event – this is particularly necessary with candidates who may be in high demand from other employers

- Double-check that all materials are available and assessors are briefed

- Confirm that the venue has full details of your booking and of your particular requirements

As nothing is left to C-H-A-N-C-E, the assessment centre is now ready to happen, like an orchestra ready to play!

# On the day

## ON THE DAY

## BEFORE THE CANDIDATES ARRIVE

As the organiser, arrive in good time at the venue and before the candidates arrive in order to:

- Check room layouts, equipment, lighting and heating levels
- Check all materials are to hand and that all technology is working
- Make sure reception staff know who is arriving and when, and that they know where to direct people. It is a good idea to put up direction signs on the walls and identify the rooms
- Be familiar with the venue facilities and procedures – wash rooms, fire escape points and fire drill arrangements
- Double-check that any special requirements or arrangements made for candidates with disabilities are in line with what has been agreed

## ON THE DAY

# WHEN THE ASSESSORS ARRIVE

Your assessors also need to arrive in good time and before the candidates:

- Assessors should be gathered together for a final briefing to check on last-minute arrangements before the candidates arrive

- They need to be familiar with their roles, their paperwork, the exercises they are running and their legal responsibilities, particularly if time has elapsed since their assessor training programme

- Assessors should also check that the rooms have been laid out to suit their requirements. If two or more assessors are involved in the same exercise, such as role-play exercises, they must agree their respective roles and activities

- They should all receive timetables and must be encouraged to stick to the times agreed. Always have an abundance of stop-watches or small clocks to distribute to them!

## ON THE DAY

# WHEN THE CANDIDATES ARRIVE

The most important first step is to set a welcoming, informative and professional tone to the candidates.

It is essential that they are briefed at the start of the assessment centre so that they feel motivated to perform as well as they can. Candidates are likely to be nervous. They may have concerns or questions which need answering but may be reluctant to air these unless encouraged to do so.

Ideally, all assessors should be introduced informally to the candidates and everyone should be wearing name badges. If pictures are taken of the candidates as an aide-memoire for the assessors, then the purpose of this should be explained clearly.

## ON THE DAY

## BRIEFING THE CANDIDATES

### TICK LIST ✓

- Thank the candidates for attending
- Introduce the assessors
- Explain house-keeping details: wash rooms, fire drills and fire escape locations
- 'Walk through' the timetable – ideally, have individual timetables available
- Remind the candidates that this is an opportunity for them to demonstrate their skills and abilities and that assessment centres are one of the fairest and most accurate ways of recruiting people to roles
- Explain how the information from the centre will be used to inform the decision-making process
- State that the day will be busy but should be enjoyable and stimulating
- Tell them how and when they will hear about the outcome and receive feedback on the results
- Remind everyone to switch off their mobile phones

## ON THE DAY

# AT THE END OF THE BRIEFING

Finally:

- Wish everyone good luck and urge them to throw themselves into the day and to contribute as much and as well as they can

- Ask the candidates to communicate any questions or concerns which they might have, or, if they are not clear at any time about what to do, to speak to any of the assessors during the day

- Check if anyone has any questions before the event begins

## ON THE DAY

## DURING THE ASSESSMENT CENTRE

As the event progresses, the organiser needs to ensure that:

- Candidates are being looked after
- The timetable is being adhered to
- Any queries from assessors and candidates are being handled
- Exercise results are being captured so that the results are available at the assessor review session

At the same time, as an assessor, you need to be:

- Completing your assessor paperwork accurately, objectively and promptly
- Sticking to your timetable

ON THE DAY

# AT THE END OF THE ASSESSMENT CENTRE

It is a good idea for all of the candidates and assessors to gather after the exercises have been completed. This is the opportunity for the assessment centre organiser to:

- Thank the candidates for their participation

- Gather any informal or formal feedback on how they found the process

- Ensure that any administration has been attended to, such as the processing of travel expenses or the reviewing of certificates of education

- Wish the candidates a safe journey home

The assessment centre organiser should also check that no paperwork or confidential materials have been left in the assessment rooms.

# Wash-up & Feedback

## WASH-UP & FEEDBACK

# IMPORTANCE OF THE REVIEW SESSION

The review session, in which the candidates' results are discussed and decisions are made, is often called a 'wash-up'. It should take place as soon as possible after the candidates have departed and the exercises have been scored.

All the information gleaned about the candidates from the exercises is put together – as if in a big washing-up bowl – reviewed in its entirety and decisions are made.

The organiser may or may not be the best person to conduct the wash-up session and the choice of the person to do this should be based upon the circumstances of the assessment centre and the styles of the individuals involved.

Whoever is running the wash-up session needs to ensure that it is given as much effort and attention as the assessment centre itself. This means that the wash-up session should be allocated a dedicated period of time to do justice to the exercise results and to the candidates' hard work.

## WASH-UP & FEEDBACK

# SETTING RULES & STANDARDS

If you are conducting the wash-up session, make sure before it begins that:

- Assessors are reminded of their responsibilities to the candidates – to be fair, objective and accurate in their scoring and their comments

- Any paperwork or scores submitted by the assessors have been fully recorded and give a clear audit trail back to the candidates' activities in the exercises – this might be interviewers' notes or candidates' written submissions

- Assessors are reminded about the competency definitions, weightings and rating scales. Any cut-offs or pass-fail marking levels which are being applied should be based on clear evidence which has linked exercise scores to actual performance on the job. They should be used with particular care and the implications of these must be stressed to assessors

- Everyone is aware that candidates have rights under the Data Protection Act to seek access to notes taken at the assessment centre about them, and that decisions can be, and sometimes are, formally challenged by candidates

## WASH-UP & FEEDBACK

# COMPLETING THE MATRIX

The exercise matrix is the focus of the review. Each candidate's scores are inserted in the appropriate exercise/competency cell to indicate how the assessor evaluated their performance in this area. See example below.

| Competencies | Verbal & numerical reasoning tests | Personality questionnaire | Group discussion | In-tray exercise | Structured competency interview | Average for competency |
|---|---|---|---|---|---|---|
| Analysis and problem solving | 4 | N/A | | 2 | | 3 |
| Commercial awareness | | | 3.5 | 5 | 2 | 3.5 |
| Decision making | | N/A | 1 | 3 | | 2 |
| Team working | | N/A | 2 | | 2 | 2 |
| Planning and organising | | N/A | | 4 | 3 | 3.5 |
| Persuasive communication | | N/A | 1 | | 3 | 2 |

N/A = not appropriate. Not given a score as it is only a secondary source of evidence. Instead, results are discussed at the assessment centre wash-up.

TOTAL 16

## WASH-UP & FEEDBACK

# EXPLORING THE CANDIDATES' RESULTS

There are different ways to capture the scores and review the results:

- Exercise by exercise
- Candidate by candidate
- Average rating for each competency (as shown on previous page)
- The average ratings for each competency, added up to make a total (again as shown on the previous page). This would then enable a rank order of candidate performance to be produced

Depending on the results of your job analysis, weightings may be applied to differentiate those competencies that are felt to have greater importance to performance in the job. If this is the case, then scores in these competencies would be adjusted accordingly (eg by a multiple of 1.5).

## WASH-UP & FEEDBACK

# CAPTURING THE WASH-UP DISCUSSIONS

Whichever method is used, if you are chairing the wash-up, it is your job to keep the assessors on-track with the quality and objectivity of their comments, to challenge them when necessary and to ask for the underpinning evidence.

- Make sure that any comments which assessors make are justifiable and accurate
- Seek quotes or examples of actual behaviour from assessors based upon observations or scores on the candidates
- Make sure assessors justify what they say

It is a good idea for someone to make a summary of the key areas discussed and to record any decisions made about each candidate. This can be either the wash-up co-ordinator or someone else appointed to the task. Avoid using one of the assessors, so they can concentrate on giving evidence.

# WASH-UP & FEEDBACK

## CAPTURING THE WASH-UP DISCUSSIONS

Use a simple form to help you such as this:

---

Name: _____

Post applied for: _____     Date of assessment centre: _____

Strengths


Development Areas


Decision:

Decline:     Hold:     Proceed to next stage/offer:

## WASH-UP & FEEDBACK

# COMMUNICATING RESULTS TO CANDIDATES

Candidates will have invested heavily in attending the assessment centre, often taking time off work to do so, and will have worked hard. As the organiser, make sure that:

- Decisions are made promptly as well as objectively and fairly

- Information on the outcome of their applications is communicated quickly to the candidates, whether successful or unsuccessful

- Your communication with unsuccessful candidates is especially sensitive – it is the least they deserve. Remember what it was like when **you** were a candidate, and how you may have wished at the time to have been better treated

## WASH-UP & FEEDBACK

# THE IMPORTANCE OF FEEDBACK

As the organiser of the assessment centre, make sure that all candidates are offered opportunities for feedback on their results.

For the successful candidates, this is an opportunity to learn about themselves and to get off to a flying start in your organisation. This is another reason why the notes and scores from an assessment centre need to be of the highest standard.

Giving effective feedback requires two-way communication with the candidate. Telephone-based or face-to-face feedback is ideal – it enables a conversation to be developed. As this may not always be possible, be careful when sending reports or scores to candidates by letter or email as these can be misinterpreted.

Above all, remember:
*Treat all **candidates** as if they were your best **customer**!*

WASH-UP & FEEDBACK

# HOW TO GIVE EFFECTIVE FEEDBACK TO CANDIDATES

Effective feedback is **POWERFUL** feedback:

**P**ositive areas and strengths should be discussed as well as developmental areas

Be **O**bjective in your comments

**W**eaknesses should be described as development areas and accompanied by practical suggestions for how to improve

Actual **E**xamples should be given based upon evidence gathered

Build **R**apport with the candidate

Be **F**ocused and clear on your messages to the candidate; be factual, but also......

Show **U**nderstanding and empathy

**L**isten to the candidate and get their views and feedback

# REVIEWING THE PROCESS

## REVIEWING THE PROCESS

## WHAT TO LOOK FOR

The final stage is to review the assessment centre process against quality and cost criteria to ensure that it is performing as well as it can and providing a return on the considerable investment involved. Show **CARE** when reviewing the process:

**C**ompetencies – are the right ones being measured? Do the definitions need revising? Do any weightings need to be applied or revised for use next time?

**A**ssessors – are they capturing information objectively? Are notes being kept of their observations? Are they using the agreed rating scale appropriately?

**R**eview – is quality time being allowed for the review session/wash-up process? Is objective accurate evidence being shared? Is an accurate record being kept of comments?

**E**xercises – are the exercises proving too difficult/too easy for the candidates? Are the exercises providing the evidence that the assessors require?

## REVIEWING THE PROCESS

## CAPTURING GOOD FEEDBACK

When reviewing your assessment centre, two major sources of information to incorporate are feedback from candidates and feedback from assessors. This can be captured either at the event itself, or shortly afterwards while it is still fresh in everyone's minds. To capture their views, you could either speak to them directly or use a questionnaire. If using a questionnaire, consider using a blend of both multiple choice and open-ended questions.

### Feedback from candidates

Ask them to comment on:

- The briefing documentation sent before the event
- The exercises – which ones were most difficult? How clear were the instructions?
- The venue
- Scheduling/timetable for the day
- Feedback they received on their performance on the day/after the event
- Any changes they would make

# REVIEWING THE PROCESS

## FEEDBACK FROM ASSESSORS

Ask them to comment on:

- The quality of their training and the briefing documentation sent to them before the event
- Clarity of the competencies
- The exercises: which ones they felt were most – and least – useful
- The venue
- Scheduling/timetable for the day
- Review/wash-up session
- Any changes they would make

## REVIEWING THE PROCESS

# CAPTURING EXERCISE RATINGS

Another important area of feedback is an analysis of the pattern of scores, awarded by the assessors, across the range of candidates and for the different exercises used. Assessment centre exercises are designed to provide a spread of scores (on the agreed rating scale) across the candidates. Reflecting this, on a typical five point scale, you would expect roughly:

- Fewer candidates to score 5 and 1 (about 5% for each)
- More to score 2 and 4 (about 25% for each)
- The rest (about 40%) to score 3

If you are not seeing a spread of scores, it could indicate:

- Exercises are too easy or too difficult
- Assessors are leaning towards the perceived 'safe' middle score rather than using the full rating scale

It is also useful to review the ratings provided by individual assessors to see if anyone is scoring either too harshly or too leniently relative to everyone else.

## REVIEWING THE PROCESS

# COLLATING & MONITORING RESULTS

Collating scores for the various exercises is worthwhile – it will enable benchmarks (often termed 'norm tables' in relation to psychometric tests) specific to your organisation to be produced, once a certain size of sample is obtained. It is also important to monitor the results for signs of adverse impact, with various groups doing less well on the exercises. Particular categories of candidate groups to monitor include gender, race, disability and age.

Consider who should capture the information and conduct the review. Someone from HR is generally best placed to monitor and collect the information. Then appoint HR and/or external consultants/a senior line manager, as appropriate, to ensure an objective review of results and subsequent implementation of the recommendations.

Evaluation relating performance on assessments to subsequent actual performance in role will allow you to gauge the centre's overall effectiveness. In some organisations, sufficient numbers of candidates (often 50 or more) will have been assessed, allowing a statistical review (or validation study) to be made. Even without enough candidates for a full-blown statistical analysis, however, it is still possible to review the success of the appointment decisions you have made.

## REVIEWING THE PROCESS

# COMPARING EXERCISE RESULTS TO OUTCOMES

- Review, on an individual basis, evaluations of appointed candidates at key milestones (for example, at the end of their probation periods or from annual performance reviews)

- Relate appointed candidates' performance, using measures such as sales figures and customer satisfaction scores, against ratings and observations made at the assessment centre – can any patterns be seen?

- Review the performance and retention of candidates taken on before the assessment centre was used, with those appointed through the assessment centre – are candidates recruited via the assessment centre performing better or staying longer than those recruited before it was used?

Reviewing your assessment centre is vital. Such a review will help you fine-tune your process, as well as give you the confidence that your organisation's investment is money well spent!

## AND FINALLY

# DEVELOPMENT CENTRES

In an assessment centre, the focus is on identifying candidates' suitability for recruitment.

While a development centre draws upon what is essentially an assessment centre approach, it has a very different objective and characteristics.

The primary objective of a development centre is:

**A focus on highlighting strengths, areas for development and how to move individuals' development forward.**

## AND FINALLY

# DEVELOPMENT CENTRES

## CHARACTERISTICS

- Still based upon competencies, but the competencies will be reflecting the future needs of the organisation and/or the participants' next career steps
- Typically of a longer duration than an assessment centre
- Language throughout will refer to observers/facilitators offering feedback to participants
- A greater emphasis on self-reflection and time for recording learning points during the event
- Face-to-face feedback to the participants on the day and/or shortly after
- The participant feedback could involve replaying video footage derived from the exercises in the development centre. This can be powerful and memorable for the participant but the costs and logistics of recording, editing and play-back need to be considered. If filming is planned, participants must be consulted beforehand and have given their agreement
- Time scheduled for individual development planning sessions either towards the end of or very shortly after the development centre
- Afterwards, follow-up activities arranged to help make development happen and to transfer learning back into the workplace

## AND FINALLY

# CONCLUSION

In this pocketbook, we have walked you through:

- The nature of assessment centres
- The benefits they bring
- How they fit into a selection process
- How to plan them, design them and run them
- How to review them for effectiveness and value for money

For an investment of time and effort, a well-designed, well-run assessment centre improves accuracy, objectivity and fairness in recruitment.

**Line managers** can become more involved and will see the benefits which will arise above and beyond an interview-only selection process.

**Candidates** appreciate that an organisation that runs an assessment centre takes its recruitment seriously.

Above all, a successful assessment centre will reflect well on you!

## About the Authors

**John Sponton, BSc Hons, PgDip, MSc, MCIPD, C.Psychol**

John is a Chartered Occupational Psychologist and Director of Informed Assessment Ltd. His career has involved roles in HR, psychometric test publishing and consultancy. He has extensive experience of the design and delivery of assessment processes for both recruitment and development. John is the co-author of Succeeding at Assessment Centres in a Week, published by Hodder and Stoughton, and Managing Recruitment Pocketbook published by Management Pocketbooks.

**Contact:** John can be contacted on 0845 606 6798 or at John.Sponton@InformedAssessment.co.uk

**Stewart Wright, BA Hons**

Stewart is a Director of Informed Assessment Ltd. Stewart worked initially in the recruitment industry, gaining a thorough background in recruitment and selection, before specialising in career management, assessment and development for an international HR consultancy. Stewart's practical experience includes the design and validation of selection processes, the design and delivery of recruitment related training workshops, selection exercise design, psychometric assessment and assessment centre management. Stewart is the co-author of Succeeding at Assessment Centres in a Week, published by Hodder and Stoughton, and Managing Recruitment Pocketbook published by Management Pocketbooks.

**Contact:** Stewart can be contacted on 0845 606 6798 or at Stewart.Wright@InformedAssessment.co.uk

## ORDER FORM

*Your details*

Name _____

Position _____

Company _____

Address _____

_____

_____

Telephone _____

Fax _____

E-mail _____

VAT No. (EC companies) _____

Your Order Ref _____

*Please send me:* | No. copies

The <u>Managing Assessment Centres</u> Pocketbook ☐

The _____ Pocketbook ☐

The _____ Pocketbook ☐

The _____ Pocketbook ☐

**Order by Post**
**MANAGEMENT**
**POCKETBOOKS LTD**
LAUREL HOUSE, STATION APPROACH,
ALRESFORD, HAMPSHIRE SO24 9JH UK

**Order by Phone, Fax or Internet**
Telephone: +44 (0)1962 735573
Facsimile: +44 (0)1962 733637
E-mail: sales@pocketbook.co.uk
Web: www.pocketbook.co.uk

*Customers in USA should contact:*
**Management Pocketbooks**
2427 Bond Street, University Park, IL 60466
Telephone: 866 620 6944   Facsimile: 708 534 7803
E-mail: mp.orders@ware-pak.com
Web: www.managementpocketbooks.com